Ex Libris

....

POP SONNETS.

POP SONNETS.

Shakespearean Spins on Your Favorite Songs.

BY

ERIK DIDRIKSEN

QUIRK BOOKS
PHILADELPHIA

Printed in China

Designed by Timothy O'Donnell
Cover illustration by Martin Hargreaves
Production management by John J. McGurk

QUIRK BOOKS
215 Church Street
Philadelphia, PA 19106
quirkbooks.com

10 9 8 7 6 5 4 3 2 1

DEDICATION

To Becca,
the left side of my brain
and the entirety of my heart

CONTENTS.

III. Songs of Time and Mortality

v.   BALLADS OF HEROES

INTRODUCTION.

ILLIAM SHAKESPEARE (1564–1616) has mystified scholars for centuries. With so little documentary evidence about his life and career, particularly in his own hand, he is a topic of endless academic speculation. Did he really compose the works attributed to him? For whom were the "Fair Youth" and "Dark Lady" sonnets written? Was Shakespeare murdered by a rival writer?

These questions, while intriguing, ignore an important aspect of Shakespeare's work. He was not an author but a *playwright*; his work is intended not to be read but *heard*. His stunning use of rhyme and rhythm not only guided the audience to greater understanding of plot and theme but also helped the actors memorize and perform his works. Given his tremendous power on the stage, we must ask ourselves: if Shakespeare's plays were intended for performance, *why do we believe his sonnets were intended solely for the page?*

In fact, they weren't. The 154 sonnets we know and cherish were an exception, written and published in 1608 to bolster his income while London theaters were closed because of plague outbreaks. His complete œuvre was far larger, encompassing thousands of unpublished sonnets that were performed with musical accompaniment between acts of his plays. These sonnets survived by being passed down orally, particularly among members of Shakespeare's troupe, the King's Men. (Said troupe endured far longer than most people realize, scoring a number one hit in 1963 with their version of "Louie, Louie.")

In 1743, Sir Kirk de Edin began transcribing these sonnets, finally providing the world with a written record of Shakespeare's lost genius. His work went largely unnoticed, however, until Columbia record executive Robert Lorre discovered the manuscripts in 1951 and began using the sonnets as the foundation for new singles. De Edin's manuscript quietly spread throughout the music industry, inspiring countless hit songs over the next sixty-five years.

The volume you hold is a selection of these lesser-known sonnets, along with the titles of the songs they helped spark. I earnestly hope they bring you a greater appreciation of both the Bard and the artists he inspired.

PART I

Sonnets of LOVE

The game of love, we intimately know —
    its laws and maxims, mastered by our hearts;
thus, I propose to be thine only beau
with passion that no other could impart.
These feelings weighing heavy in my breast
should in thy soul be similarly sown;
and now they all are earnestly express'd
so that my vows are understood and known:
O, never shall I vacate from thy side,
nor ever shall I disappoint thee hence,
nor will the day approach that wounded pride
shall rise from some unfaithful dalliance.
    — My actions leave thy face unstained by tears
        and ledgers of my lies shall remain clear.

Rick Astley, "Never Gonna Give You Up"

Into the well, I cast a humble pray'r
and though I'll not reveal the wish I made,
our eyes, they met and we a moment shar'd,
wherein my silent want was well-convey'd.
Before we met, I had no yearnings borne
for fairytale romance or courtship's glee,
but O! the summer breeze! thy breeches torn!
I have no doubt thou art my destiny!
Though we've each other only moments known,
my heart doth fling fair Logic now away!
I beg thee, take my favor for thine own —
perchance to call upon me soon, I pray!
   — For long before we had a chance to start,
      thy absence left an aching in my heart.

Carly Rae Jepsen, "Call Me Maybe"

Thou art a flame that burns within my breast,
      the singular desire within my heart.
Believe my wish, most solemnly profess'd,
that we should ne'er again be made apart.
Yet we are twain; it seems thou'rt worlds away —
I cannot reach thee with my outstretch'd hand
to soothe thy aching soul if thou shouldst say
thy heart had other circumstances plann'd.
Pray speak of why our love such torment holds,
and prithee say why this must folly be!
No, tell me not; I fear what might unfold
if our two fondest hopes should not agree.
   — I cannot hold my passion long at bay
      for I do want love fashion'd strong that way.

Backstreet Boys, "I Want It That Way"

Thy confidence in Nature's gifts is strain'd;
  I know not why, for thine's a pleasing face.
Pray, witness all the staring unconstrain'd
by those who mark thine entrance to a place.
Thy naked face is beauty unsurpass'd;
thy countenance is not by rouge improv'd.
Like Helen's, it could launch a navy vast,
yet thy reflection leaves thee still unmov'd.
My life, once dark, is bathed in brilliant light
for thou hast graced it with thy presence sweet;
yet thou'lt not see the passion thou'st ignite
when thou hast fix'd thy gaze upon thy feet.
  — Thy charms are temper'd with humility,
    and make thee still more beautiful to me.

One Direction, "What Makes You Beautiful"

Each night I close my eyes to sleep, assured
that in my dreams I'll see once more thy face;
and thus I know thy soul hath still endur'd
beyond this world's ephemeral embrace.
I know not if thy soul stays at my side
or if it every night from Heaven leaves.
No matter where it lives, thy love abides
within me, and again there life achieves.
Thy presence hath my courage wholly steel'd;
thy spirit's overtaken all my fears.
To Father Time our love will never yield;
it shall remain unshaken o'er the years.
  — Although thy image fades at th' break of dawn,
    my heart, with thee inside, will e'er go on.

Celine Dion, "My Heart Will Go On"

An action imperceptible to most
doth rend my heart when thou dost it perform;
while I am pain'd to look, I'm still engross'd —
and while my heart is broken, so it's warm'd.
Thou knowèst not the suff'ring I've endured,
the fruitless struggle to forget thy face —
but I shall e'er remember, I'm assured,
so long as thou repeat'st that tiny grace.
If I cannot escape thy minute charms,
I'll win thy love and bring thee endless bliss;
I long to hold thee tightly in my arms
and bring thee happiness with ev'ry kiss.
     — The love I hold for thee shall ne'er be lost
       so long as thou shalt do that thing thou dost.

The Wonders, "That Thing You Do!"

My mistress' eyes are nothing like the stars;
they've brighter shine than all those overhead.
Her hair's cascade her visage never mars
but effortlessly frames her face instead.
And yet, if I should tell her what I see —
that she hath been by Aphrodite bless'd —
she'd quietly demur and disagree
and I shall with these words sincere protest:
"When I observe thy countenance's grace,
I see no fault — no flaw one might repair;
and when a smile doth blossom 'cross thy face,
the world takes heed and stops to fondly stare.
   — No words could e'er sufficiently impart
      all thy perfection, just the way thou art."

Bruno Mars, "Just the Way You Are"

I feel I've been for ages long interr'd,
companionless a hundred years or more;
and though thy sly advances interest stirr'd,
that dost not my return'd desire ensure.
I shan't engage thy passions straightaway,
although my body yearns for thine embrace;
my heart hath temper'd its impulsive ways
and settled me to take a slower pace.
I'll grant thy wish, if thou dost demonstrate
thy valor and make thy impression well.
I may thy hungers prurient well-sate
if in reciprocation thou'st excel.
   — I am a genie in this lamp confined;
      release me if thy heart is so inclined.

Christina Aguilera, "Genie in a Bottle"

I shall not care if ev'ry single week
begins with Monday wrapp'd in dismal blue
with Tuesday trailing after, looking bleak
in ashen gray, completely without hue.
On Wednesday morns, the gloomy break of dawn
may hoist the forlorn flag and follow suit.
Though Thursday wilt for too long linger on,
I'll lie in wait for what's in hot pursuit.
How Saturday turns briskly into night!
The Sabbath time will far too quickly race
through ev'ry moment bringing me delight
within my dear beloved's fond embrace.
    — As th' weekend starts, I thank the Lord above:
        'tis Friday now, and truly I'm in love.

The Cure, "Friday I'm in Love"

Throughout my body, I feel sudden chills
  but they spring not from newly fallen snow;
instead, they stem from each romantic thrill
that being in thy presence doth bestow.
I must the call for self-improvement heed;
to be a better man, I'll swiftly learn
for I must be the one to meet thy needs —
the lord for whom my lady's soul doth yearn.
And so, if I thy tender heart have warm'd
and made myself the one thou hast ador'd,
I'll prove I have my character transform'd
and evermore thy faith in me reward.
  — There are no further words I'll e'er require:
    my dear, thou art the one I do desire.

John Travolta and Olivia Newton-John,
"You're the One That I Want"

I had considered love a mythic force,
   a fable told to children ere they slept —
and if 'twas real, it show'd me no remorse
while it withheld the wistful dreams I kept.
I thought of romance like a chest of gold,
assuming what I gave would e'er be lost;
thus I commanded that my heart grow cold
so I might ne'er incur its heavy cost.
But when at last I saw her visage fair,
my chill'd convictions thaw'd to my relief;
I'm now the heart's disciple, deep in pray'r
and thoroughly devout in my belief.
   — No force on earth could ever be applied
      to make me, love's apostle, leave her side.

The Monkees, "I'm a Believer"

I know not where this tender love was birth'd,
though I have watch'd it through the seasons grow.
The winter broke to flow'ring o'er the earth
and passion blossom'd in the melting snow.
These summer nights still seem of heat devoid;
the darkness threatens harsh and bitter harm.
And yet, our love doth fill the endless void;
I feel no worry held within thy arms.
There is a gentle warmth in thine embrace
that brings my spirit true romantic bliss;
I'll reach my hand t'ward thine in hope to trace
each other's heart with holy palmers' kiss.
   — In truth I vow there's been no better time
      than spent with thee, my sweetest Caroline!

Neil Diamond, "Sweet Caroline"

Herodotus's works I've not perus'd;
I know so little from his Histories.
Geography doth render me confus'd,
for I've learn'd naught from Eratosthenes.
I'm ignorant of scientific law
and all the lessons that it doth purvey;
I'd doubtlessly commit some great *faux pas*
if I attempted *à parler français.*
Yet I am not of scholarship devoid;
I've master'd all the sage philosophy
within the only field I'll not avoid —
my singular devotedness to thee.
   — If thou shouldst love me true with all thy heart,
     no greater wonder could this world impart.

Sam Cooke, "Wonderful World"

Wherefore should friends of mine besmirch thy name?
They've laughed at our rapport and cruelly jok'd.
We've caused them no offense, thus share no blame;
their violence comes completely unprovoked.
Let not their slanders weigh upon thy mind,
for we shall to each other faithful be.
They claim we look absurd; they must be blind,
for I a truly gorgeous vision see!
Reflection's image shows me the trouvère
who sang how Peggy Sue his heart beguiled;
and lo! Thy countenance doth well compare
with she who turn'd the world on with her smile.
   — So let them say about us what they want,
     for I care not about their boorish taunts.

Weezer, "Buddy Holly"

Her smile, it doth recall a simpler time —
the bygone years when I was but a boy;
each day held some discovery sublime,
each exploration brought some newfound joy.
When I upon her charming visage gaze,
my mind o'erflows with memories I keep —
the images of those idyllic days
stir up my soul and make me fondly weep.
Her azure eyes, so bright and sunny, ought
to be preserv'd from ev'ry ounce of grief,
just as her hair recalls the haven sought
when from the storm I needed some relief.
   — I hope thy heart I've equally beguil'd —
      so where shall we now go, my sweetest child?

Guns N' Roses, "Sweet Child o' Mine"

These verses I shall fondly dedicate
  to nobles who from wealthy peerage hail.
Their gold buys wine and frippery ornate;
they travel much, but ne'er in steerage sail.
I hold my heart for one of such repute;
for such a lord, I've sav'd each sweet embrace —
so if thou seek'st his love, our fierce dispute
shall be resolv'd with blows across thy face.
Behold! I shall this gentleman seduce:
I'll compliment his vestments and his air
before I have myself well introduced,
a woman of esteem beyond compare.
  — The booming sound of drumming he shall hear
    will be my heart's deep cadence when he's near.

Nicki Minaj, "Super Bass"

P ray do not turn that crimson lantern on
    or paint that vulgar rouge across thy face;
thou needest not those bawdy vestments don
nor with that ruddy brush thy cheeks debase.
I beg thee to this sordid life forego:
turn not a trick, but prithee turn the page!
O, dear Roxanne, thou dost not need to go
into that den of sin to earn thy wage.
Thou know'st I'll never to thee condescend;
yet I must now express my deep regret
if thou shouldst there another moment spend,
for I have loved thee since the hour we met.
  — No longer shall I share thee with the night;
    I beg of thee, snuff out thy scarlet light.

The Police, "Roxanne"

Upon my heart thou hold'st a rightful claim —
a vow that distance shan't our friendship breach;
and though I've garnered ample wealth and fame,
we have maintain'd our closeness unimpeach'd.
With thee, companion true, I'll share my lot
and make our fortunes evermore entwined —
for in the dark of night the eyes cannot
observe the treasures they'd in daylight find.
But from the heart we shine like beacons bright;
our bond's been strengthen'd by the oaths we swore
to persevere — to stand firm and unite
when life sends storm clouds threatening to pour.
   — Thou needest not be drench'd when showers fall;
     pray take thy place beneath my parasol.

Rihanna, featuring Jay-Z, "Umbrella"

Such mem'ries wait where once our love did grow
soaked all with rain. How quickly we'd descend
into the forested ravine below
to dance and play in th' mists of dawn, sweet friend!
Yet, Father Time must always onward march;
he leaves behind each joyful afternoon
beneath the sun, behind the rainbow's arch,
near creeks where we'd our youthful laughter strewn.
Yet while each day doth further from us drift,
each glimpse of thee doth bring me fresh delight.
I see the years endow'd thee well with gifts
that do new passions in my breast ignite.
   — I long to bed thee in the verdant grass
      and call thee evermore my brown-eyed lass.

Van Morrison, "Brown-Eyed Girl"

Two noblemen before thee genuflect,
    entreating thee in earnest for thy hand.
The first, he garners riches and respect;
the other's only flights of fancy plann'd.
The prince with wealth, his pockets overflow
with jewels amass'd from mercantile success;
the life this prosp'rous merchant could bestow
would make thy father dear your union bless.
His eyes instead would well up with regret
if thou shouldst pick me as thy groom instead;
I'm not of any noble birth, and yet
I'd be the truer love, if we should wed.
    — By epithets, perhaps, or flow'ry prose,
        I'll treasure all thy love how it's disclosed.

Spin Doctors, "Two Princes"

Each morning, ere I rouse myself from sleep,
I'm bless'd to know I'm with thee when thou wak'st;
and I shall be the company thou'st keep
beside thee on each journey that thou tak'st.
At night, when to the public-house I've gone,
it is to quaff down mugs of ale with thee;
and when incessantly I prattle on,
thou find'st the patience to attentive be.
For thee, I would endure a journey great —
on foot I would embark five hundred miles
and verily, I'd not then slow my gait;
I'd walk it o'er again to see thee smile.
  — And once I'd walk'd the full three hundred leagues,
    I'd be thy love, collapsèd from fatigue.

The Proclaimers, "I'm Gonna Be (500 Miles)"

PART II

Sonnets of DESPAIR

NOS SEPARABIT AMOR

I have reflected on my sad mistake
  that's wounded thee and caused tremendous grief;
my deeds have led thy eager heart to break
by lulling thee into a false belief.
Flirtation's charms do often love portend,
and yet provide thee with no guarantee;
I thought thou wouldst account, my dearest friend,
for how mercurial my moods may be.
Alas! Instead, I once again have erred
by playing with thy passions just for sport.
Alack-a-day! Thou thinkest that I cared
so deeply that I was for thee to court.
  — Thou thinkest I'm thy angel, void of sin,
    but I hold no such innocence within.

Britney Spears, "Oops! I Did It Again"

A gentle friend whom I have long adored
hath been a steadfast comrade at my side;
and yet, of late, I sense that our accord
is weaken'd by my deeply wounded pride.
The cause is far too easy to detect:
he hath a courtship with a lass begun;
and though our bond fraternal I respect,
I wish that I instead her heart had won.
How fortunate to gaze into her eyes!
and how divine her soft embrace must be!
Imagining his arms about his prize
doth fill my heart with pain and jealousy.
   — For Jessie's winsome girl I long have pined;
      pray, tell me where I'll such a woman find!

Rick Springfield, "Jessie's Girl"

My mem'ry gazes back on young romance
and on its twilight throes, when first thou left;
thou claim'd we needed absence to advance
but for togetherness, we'd been bereft.
Thou soon return'd, thy face forlorn and drawn,
and from thy lips hung promises to change;
then, by the morrow, all those oaths were gone
and once again we found ourselves estranged.
The cycle never breaks; our sordid tales
end always with ellipses, not full stops.
When yesternight our courtship freshly fail'd,
thou saw'st the cue to take it from the top.
   — But now that we are once again apart,
      I swear thou'lt ne'er again reclaim my heart.

Taylor Swift, "We Are Never Ever Getting Back Together"

I notice my belovèd on thy arm,
and from my lips I spit a vulgar oath.
My want of wealth has caus'd my courtship harm,
and so I've lost my love; fie on you both!
The realization aches within my heart
that I'd be hers if I'd a larger purse;
and yet, a gentle blessing I impart —
though it's embedded in a vile curse.
Forgive my sin, that I no stallion own,
but I've no want of transport with my mule.
Thou surely hast the greater riches shown,
but that doth not forgive my treatment cruel.
    — I pity thee; thy romance shall not last
        if thou hast insufficient gold amass'd.

CeeLo Green, "F**k You!"

O soothe thy anxious nerves and halt thy tongue!
Compose thyself and see the simple truth:
with me thou art sincere, and yet among
a group of peers, thou swiftly turn'd uncouth.
Thy manner is affected, and thine eyes
gaze o'er thy shoulder with conceal'd unease.
Thy stilted efforts make a poor disguise;
'tis foolish, trying all the world to please!
Why must thou complicate our sacred trust,
imprudently obscuring thy true grace?
I only feel frustration and disgust
when seeing thy real beauty so debased.
— Thy nature's forged by hardships overthrown;
    pray make thy public character thine own.

Avril Lavigne, "Complicated"

Thou art amongst a group of oafish louts
who speak at length of how you should'st receive
what you desir'st; and yet, you layabouts
do nothing to such lofty goals achieve.
Thus I'll not tell thee where I do reside
that thou mightst send thy couriers to me;
thy overtures for time are here denied,
for never shall I rendezvous with thee.
I want thee not, nor any of thy kind,
for you're unworthy to my love procure;
I warrant better than the unrefined
approach thou takèst to my heart secure.
   — No suitor's vows of love shall I attend
      deliver'd from the carriage of his friend.

TLC, "No Scrubs"

O hear this tale of misery and pain —
a melancholic man with broken pride
is curs'd with an affliction thus explain'd:
he lacks a friend in whom he can confide.
A monochromatism of the mind
doth plague his spirit, changing what he sees.
No matter where he looks, he cannot find
the pleasant verdant color of the trees,
nor any crimson in his lover's lips.
His house, his steed, his clothes — his mind as well —
they all have had their color cruelly stripp'd
and left a dark and dismal cobalt shell.
   — Now all that's left's a solitary hue;
     and all he sees — and ere shall be — is blue.

Eiffel 65, "Blue (Da Ba Dee)"

This morn I woke and donn'd my finest clothes,
  uneasy for the social call I plann'd;
I sought paternal blessings to propose
so I might ask thy daughter for her hand.
My case was made with kindness and respect,
yet found my pleas were hastily subdued —
not only had my hopes been wholly wreck'd,
'twas in a manner churlish, brusque, and rude.
Thou surely knowest I too am a man;
why must thou play the part of boorish brute?
This insult shall not be a perm'nent ban;
thy surly prohibitions I'll refute.
  — To venerate our love, despite thy strife,
    I'll cherish true thy daughter as my wife.

Magic!, "Rude"

Sometimes I feel I should decisions make
to flee the grievous romance that we keep.
The torment I've endured keeps me awake,
and life's confounded with so little sleep.
In bygone days, I ran into thy arms
for I believed our love was pure and sweet,
but now I know the power of thy charms
and how I should instead from thee retreat.
I gave to thee what passion I possess'd;
'twas not enough to slake thy callous thirst,
for now thou drink'st the tears that do express
the ceaseless pain of courtship cruelly curs'd.
   — Thou claim'st divinity's in am'rous pray'r,
      and yet our love's been tainted past compare.

Soft Cell, "Tainted Love"

W hat thou requir'st, I harbor deep inside —
I too possess the things for which thou yearn'st.
So if thou want'st these hungers slak'd, my pride
should not be injur'd fast when thou return'st.
I shall not cuckold thee or break thy trust;
my wish is not to leave my lover spurn'd.
But if I will not satiate my lust,
I should be shown the deep regard I've earn'd.
'Tis true, thy kisses are like honey sweet,
but so's the gold that doth my coffers fill.
I have no need to once again entreat
thee to be shown a shred of thy good will.
    — And so, good sir, do not my heart neglect;
        when thou com'st home, pray show me some respect.

Aretha Franklin, "Respect"

Dear friend, hast thou a moment to attend
my lamentations piteous and sad?
I'll fuss o'er everything, from start to end —
and nothingness as well, for I've gone mad.
I've found I have a histrionic streak —
my choler doth submerge my weary soul
and melancholy makes my outlook bleak
for o'er my humors I've lost all control.
At times, I find that I hallucinate;
at others, I've myself wholly dismay'd.
These awful maladies accumulate
and cause my spirit's ruin and decay.
   — O, do I suffer truest lunacy,
      or hath my pipe's effects new potency?

Green Day, "Basket Case"

My dearest, settle thy uncertain mind
and tell me the conclusion thou hast reach'd!
Will I from here abscond, or shalt thou find
me fit to loiter 'round here unimpeach'd?
If thou wouldst say I am thy lover true,
I'll here until the end of days persist;
O prithee say if our romance is through,
so I can leave if I have been dismiss'd.
Thou hast my tortured begging well enjoy'd —
thy teasing's brought thy soul a cruel delight.
It's made my days much darker than the void,
when prior days had been so warm and bright.
   — Pray share the disposition of thy heart:
      shall I remain or should I now depart?

The Clash, "Should I Stay or Should I Go?"

When I am of companionship bereft
and in my breast a melancholy swells,
I feel the only ally I have left
is this, the coastal city where I dwell.
Her crowded streets my ev'ry step embrace
as I through all her rolling hills proceed.
The ocean's breeze doth kiss my weary face
and weeps with me for ev'ry dark misdeed.
Recalling all the agonies I've braved,
I wish to ne'er again feel such dismay;
I bid thee, take me where I shall be saved —
with those I love, I shall not go astray.
   — Beneath the bridge, I struggled to abate
     the endless hunger I could never sate.

Red Hot Chili Peppers, "Under the Bridge"

My heart's a scale that measures love and hate,
each in the full supply I hold for thee —
and though the malice hath tremendous weight,
I find it's counterbalanced perfectly.
Thy base transgressions can't be wiped away,
and yet I wish to pardon ev'ry crime.
Thy presence strains my nerves; why must thou stay
and make confus'd the shameful and sublime?
My mind retreats up to the twinkling stars
instead of holding fast to what is wise;
I dream of days before our love was marred
by infidelities and sordid lies
    — too fanciful to count them, should we part,
       the problems swift subtracted from my heart.

Ariana Grande, featuring Iggy Azalea, "Problem"

When first we fell apart, I fill'd with fear
that life without thy love could not be led,
but through my long reflections 'pon my tears,
I fill'd myself with courage in its stead.
Yet thou return'st and for my love implore
with weary sadness hung upon thy brow.
(O, how I would have bolted tight my door
if I had known thou'dst be returning now!)
But without bolts, I beckon thee to leave —
thou hast no welcome place, and thus must go.
Thou'st fled and then expected me to grieve
and crumble like the Walls of Jericho;
   — yet I shall live and boldly rise above
      so long as I know how to give my love.

Gloria Gaynor, "I Will Survive"

My darling, I a true dilemma face:
thy heart endeavors to my love estrange,
but I possess no power to replace
its warmth, or to thy callous'd viewpoint change.
My mother doth my sordid fears dismiss;
she urges me to give my hand to one
who surely would deserve my loving kiss —
yet thou hast my affections truly won.
I beg thee, see these tears upon my cheek
and hear the soft entreatments I have made!
If thou canst not of honest passion speak,
then hide thy feelings in a masquerade.
   — Convince me love's return'd in equal share;
     for thou'rt the only one for whom I'll care.

The Cardigans, "Lovefool"

The fluctuating spins of Fortune's wheel
do oft portend the shocking and arcane;
and yet those times unlikely and surreal
are far outnumber'd by the mere mundane.
'Tis not unusual to courted be;
to spend thy time with suitors is not rare —
although 'tis not uncommon then to see
my tearful face, unveiling my despair.
If thou shouldst e'er desire a perfect love,
pray know 'tis not so singular a thirst;
for daily is it pray'd to God above
by those who unrequited love have nurs'd.
  — So if thy wooers leave thy bosom cold,
    be not surprised that love for thee I hold.

Tom Jones, "It's Not Unusual"

S he spoke of love as though it were a tree —
 how passion's strengths are in its common roots;
and since we hold no commonality,
the sapling withers, bearing us no fruit.
Our lives, she said, have kept our souls apart;
our diff'rences have courtship's bliss deterr'd.
Yet I believed I still could win her heart
if I discover'd where our minds concurred.
So I inquir'd of that comedy
we'd seen upon the stage one autumn night:
its winsome lead and witty repartee —
it surely must have brought her soul delight!
  — Our mutual enjoyment she'd concede,
     thus planting courtship's delicate new seed.

Deep Blue Something, "Breakfast at Tiffany's"

I found my way into the market square
to drink in deep the festival's delights.
I suffered the misfortune of you there
just as I'd borne through all our troubled nights.
So recently we broke the bonds of love,
I doubted you had sooner still forgot;
yet still your jealous anger rose above
for when another's passions had grown hot.
Yes, I am in his gaze, and he in mine,
but your eyes somewhere else should swiftly start.
For three long years, I 'llowed myself to pine
for matrimony's gifts to grace my heart.
    — If truly you did wish to win my hand,
      you should have graced it with a wedding band.

Beyoncé, "Single Ladies (Put a Ring on It)"

If on the morrow I should here depart,
wouldst thou recall with wistfulness my face?
My soul demands I new adventures start;
I must abscond from this familiar place.
I've ne'er known sweeter love in all my days,
yet still my spirit craves the unexplor'd.
Make no attempt to curb my wand'ring ways;
'twould only serve to injure our accord.
I beg thee, feel no shame or deep remorse,
for on my shoulders weighs this heavy blame.
Still I cannot refuse the flighty course
my heart hath set; I'll not be render'd tame.
   — O, since I'll ne'er domesticated be,
      I'll fly forevermore, unbound and free!

Lynyrd Skynyrd, "Free Bird"

I n ev'ry prior time when thou had ask'd
about my day, I'd plainly be address'd.
Thy sentiments hath ne'er before been mask'd,
yet now it seems there's something unexpress'd.
O love untrue, thy words betray thy crimes!
Thy answers lack the tender sobriquets
thou freely spak'st so many other times —
as if to hide thy sins and sad regrets.
Hast thou a strumpet to thy dwelling brought?
I cannot be so easily misled!
If thou art guilty, I've thee simply caught
by hearing all the words thou'st left unsaid.
  — And so, if thou art innocent of blame,
    then prove thy conscience clear and say my name.

Destiny's Child, "Say My Name"

PART III

Songs of
TIME AND
MORTALITY

Thou mayst awaken in a cottage small
    or in some yet unvisited new land;
thou mayest dwell within a lavish hall,
where thou dost take a stunning woman's hand.
If thou shouldst find this life is not a dream
and question how thou cam'st to lead this life:
"This place is not my home," thou'lt surely scream —
"nor is this gorgeous woman here my wife!"
Yea, thou shalt question all that Fate hath wrought:
how this became thy home, or th' hand thou'st won —
and this endeavor's further questions brought!
Thy greatest plea's to God: "What have I done?"
    — But time's swift current flows as e'er it does;
        and all's the same, just as it ever was.

Talking Heads, "Once in a Lifetime"

A lonely maiden from a hamlet small;
a boy within a woeful city rear'd —
they both at midnight left their ports of call
t'ward any destination volunteer'd.
A public-house is where their journeys end,
where patrons' pipes burn long and minstrels play.
The darken'd hours have made them more than friends,
the other's smile inviting each to stay.
Look ye on those who wander through the streets
beneath the lamplight, searching for a soul —
they comb the darken'd night in hope to meet
the sweet companion that shall make them whole.
  — Ensure thy heart won't let their spirit leave;
    'tis most important thou dost e'er believe.

Journey, "Don't Stop Believin'"

Young Thomas is a longshoreman by trade
whose guild ceas'd work to fight for wages fair.
The strike drags on; 'tis weeks since he's been paid —
a crawl t'ward destitution and despair.
But he hath been from truest hardship saved;
his sweetheart Gina's at an inn employ'd
where, for her love, she works as though enslaved
so they might still their usurers avoid.
She tells him softly, "We must not despair;
despite our prospects grim, we must endure!
We have our love; 'tis wealth beyond compare,
worth all the trials of our fate unsure.
   — With pray'r alone, we have survived 'til now.
     Pray take my hand and we'll prevail somehow!"

Bon Jovi, "Livin' on a Prayer"

An ancient man of preternatural health
upon his birthday won a princely prize;
but ere he could enjoy his sudden wealth,
the touch of death forever clos'd his eyes.
A timid man embark'd a sailing ship,
although his fear of water was renown'd;
he spoke of how he revel'd in the trip
as th' vessel sank beneath him and he drown'd.
The hand of Fate is mischievous and sly;
it plays its sordid games with all our lives —
decanting wine to come across a fly,
a thousand spoons when one requires knives.
   — To learn thy future, read not leaves of tea;
     for all our fortune's steep'd in irony.

Alanis Morissette, "Ironic"

W hen waking on a morn depriv'd of sun,
    I call'd upon the local troubadour
and, telling him the day hath not begun,
requested then a solemn song of yore.
The tune did send my mem'ry to the past
to look on faces I'd not lately seen;
and whilst into the depths my thoughts were cast,
the faces came with clarity pristine.
As all these old emotions ebb and swell,
I float on mem'ry's seas; the course I chart
is t'ward the recollection o' which I dwell —
of Marianne, and how she did depart.
    — O, music's to my heart a healing song,
        and is far more than just a feeling strong.

Boston, "More Than a Feeling"

O hast thou felt the tragic touch of Fate,
  or art thou kin with those who've borne its curse?
Pray hast thou e'er collaps'd beneath the weight
of dreadful circumstances growing worse?
While I believe I have no coward's heart,
I've ne'er endured a trial of my pluck;
I fear what such adversity'd impart,
and thus I'm grateful for my sterling luck.
I've ne'er been tempted to my knuckles rap
on timber to my fortunes good preserve;
and those I know who've fallen 'to that trap
have suffer'd more than e'er they did deserve.
  — I'm glad I'm not by knocking's magic stain'd,
    for that's the frank impression I've obtain'd.

The Mighty Mighty Bosstones, "The Impression That I Get"

I'll not be made a cuckold by my miss,
and of this fact, she hath me well assur'd.
Yet this does not assure domestic bliss –
she may, for honor's sake, have woe endur'd.
The lessons of our forebears shall impart
the ways to keep a marriage well content;
for in this fleeting life, what sets apart
true love from all the world, impermanent?
Thine eyes have glaz'd, as though thou'rt in a trance;
my musings philosophical grow old,
and since thou want'st no doctrine now but dance,
I'll music make — not cool, but icy cold.
   — So ladies! though the rough winds blown away,
     pray shake it like the darling buds of May.

Outkast, "Hey Ya!"

M y eyes have ne'er a precious stone appraised;
I've only seen what pictures do depict.
I hold no pride for places I was raised,
for they exist, depress'd and derelict.
Yet I've met souls in whom a hunger's stirr'd
for riches and adventures past compare —
the troubadours they hear, with notes and words,
inspire them to take decadent airs
with wines expensive, carriages ornate.
This sort of life is well beyond my reach,
but I do not lament its latent fate
for I'll not heed the lessons minstrels preach.
    — Instead, I'll reign as queen of my own hive
        where dreams of earnest happiness shall thrive.

Lorde, "Royals"

This mountainside, engulf'd in snow untouch'd,
  reveals the isolation I command;
the icy storms that I once tightly clutch'd
within my heart are blanketing the land.
No longer could I heed my parents' will
to hold my youthful hopes and fears at bay;
so all have seen I've mastered winter's chill —
my years of forced seclusion toss'd away.
The page hath now been turn'd; I'll break the chains
that kept restrain'd my true identity.
This queen will rule, but o'er her own domain,
without a care for what they think of me.
  — I'll not again the falling snow withhold,
    for I have ne'er been bothered by the cold.

Idina Menzel, "Let It Go"

O there are tasks impossible to bring
  to resolution by a person's choice:
the hymns that only cherubim can sing
cannot be sounded by a mortal voice,
nor can the objects that cannot be made
be fashion'd by the work of human hands,
nor can'st thou come to any victim's aid
if that should contradict cruel Fate's commands.
But waste no tears for what thou can't pursue,
for there are ventures greater still than these.
To live — to care — to thine own self be true —
all noble occupations done with ease
  — if thou art guided by the simple creed
    that love is all thy life doth truly need.

The Beatles, "All You Need Is Love"

O I have climb'd the tallest mountain's peak
and sprinted 'cross the meadow's open berth;
I have surmounted high stone walls to seek
a love divine whilst I still walk the earth.
With pilgrim's lips, I've kiss'd a maiden sweet
and felt my soul restor'd as we embrac'd.
With seraphim, I've dialogues complete;
with demons, I've our fingers interlac'd.
Yes, I accept our Savior shall return
to render judgment and absolve the pure;
yet in my unchain'd heart such fires burn —
I ceaseless trek t'ward what I'm hunting for.
    — I've listen'd to the sermons preach'd in church —
        still I've not found the faith for which I search.

U2, "I Still Haven't Found What I'm Looking For"

Thou knowest what a falsehood it would be
  and how my word could no more be believ'd
if I were fool enough to here decree
that we still greater heights could yet achieve.
No, we've soar'd higher than the tow'ring flames
that burn the treetops, high into the night.
We shall not fall; instead, we'll take our aim
at the pursuit of physical delights.
No more shall we take time to hem and haw,
nor shall we e'er again the marshland wade —
for there our love, within its swampy maw,
would be into a fun'ral pyre made.
  — The doors of chaste perception we have raz'd;
    unfetter'd we shall set the night ablaze.

The Doors, "Light My Fire"

The toy shoppe's where our shillings few were spent;
we laugh'd together like a pair of loons
as we observ'd the delicate ascent
of nine and ninety crimson air-balloons.
An army watchman, looking t'ward the skies,
mistook the floating spheres for tools of war;
he raised his voice and sounded urgent cries —
a call to arms to rouse the mighty corps.
With lightning speed, the infantry was rais'd
and call'd to battle by the trumpets' sound;
within a wink, they had our village raz'd —
our humble hamlet burnèd to the ground.
   — One last balloon I'll wistfully release
      amongst the ashes, praying hard for peace.

Nena, "99 Luftballons"

My path through life persistently is blazed
without a torch to light the darken'd way.
Instead I march, undaunted and unfazed,
to follow courses that my heart surveys.
I know not where the drumming in my chest
will lead, for I'm bereft of maps or charts;
the only knowledge of this thrilling quest
I hold is where the high adventure starts.
The elders claim my life is toss'd away
on dreams befitting simpletons and fools;
if Father Time should pass me, as they say,
I gladly will surrender to his rule.
   — So wake me not — I'll dream at any cost,
     for those who wander are not always lost.

Avicii, featuring Aloe Blacc, "Wake Me Up"

From observation of my gallant gait
and its effects upon the sex so fair,
thou see'st no hope for discourse or debate,
for comely ladies find me debonair.
Though music fills my ears with pleasing sound
and pleasant women company provide,
I often find myself upon the ground
when Providence hath cast her wings aside.
I shall not feel discouraged or abus'd
if you should find your gaze averted hence;
I'll fit my thoughts to all the printed news
and its effects upon us learnèd gents.
— No matter what it says, we all must strive
to pass each of our days truly alive.

The Bee Gees, "Stayin' Alive"

The beach is bare; the bathers all have left,
    for autumn's cool pervades the summer air.
I trek across this town of souls bereft
to pass thy home, although thou art not there.
Yet, in my mem'ry's eye, I see thee still —
thy shining auburn hair, thy sun-kiss'd skin.
Each precious thought recall'd returns the thrill
thy presence render'd to my heart within.
Still, they are only mem'ries in my mind;
those bygone days are now forever pass'd,
but I'll remain to those sweet days resigned,
reliving recollections I've amass'd.
    — I know my love for thee shall e'er live on,
        e'en once the boys of summer all have gone.

Don Henley, "The Boys of Summer"

PART IV

ROGUES, RASCALS

AND

WANTON WOMEN

O Jenny sweet, I'll turn to only thee;
   for me, thy fond caress's the salve prescrib'd.
I'm not like other lads who look'd to see
thy name upon the whitewash'd boards inscrib'd.
Yea, there was further writing on the wall,
a message that such wond'rous prospects show'd:
those oracle's words — "For a good time, call" —
and seven figures, like some type of code.
I'm gladden'd by thy smile and numbers strange,
although thou hast my visage never seen.
Do not thy mathematic cipher change,
and I will make thee evermore my queen!
   — I know the sequence that shall make thee mine:
      'tis eight six seven, five three zero nine.

Tommy Tutone, "867-5309/Jenny"

M y honor won't be tarnish'd with a lie,
nor will my brothers' — here's our common truth:
the female form doth often catch our eye
below the waist (if I may be uncouth)!
My gaze transfix'd upon her petticoat,
I think of how I'd woo this woman grand;
I'd to her ev'ry wish myself devote
in hopes I might win more than just her hand.
The maidens sporting more beneath their skirts
have in my breast a lusty feeling stirr'd;
thus, I defy the cretins who assert
the flatter fanny is the one preferr'd!
— So let us all our preference delcare:
three cheers for the well-rounded derrière!

Sir Mix-a-Lot, "Baby Got Back"

If thou art late for lessons when thou'st rise,
thy mother shall not let thee truant be;
thou must attend thy tutor pros'lytize
his lecture like some zealous homily.
When thou return'st, thy property's been lost —
thy parents have their own misdeeds ignor'd;
they have thy pipe into the rubbish toss'd,
along with carnal drawings well-adored.
They threaten to detain thee o'er attire,
then promise to evict thee for thy hair!
Thy fav'rite minstrels draw their bitter ire
(though I detect some envy in their glare).
— Kneel not before authority; instead,
    defend thy right to paint the city red!

Beastie Boys, "(*You Gotta*) *Fight for Your Right* (*to Party!*)"

Tonight such festive music we shall play
 to bring your evening unabash'd delight!
We hope your inhibitions to allay
so you can freely revel in the night.
Pray lift yourselves, rise from your wretch'd seats!
Pavanne without restraint; O, be not shy!
Yea, feel within thy soul the rhythmic beat
and galliard with hands raised t'ward the sky!
Be not afraid of forming joyous throngs
so unreservedly, you seem run mad.
If you'd gavotte away the whole night long,
our foolish hearts should truly be made glad!
 — No matter what each turn of Fate may bring,
  we shall through ev'ry day be shuffling.

LMFAO, "Party Rock Anthem"

In summer's heat, thy absence left me chill'd
with fitful feelings tugging at my heart.
Uneasy, restless, desp'rate to be thrill'd,
I sought a jaunt about within my cart.
As I approached a bridge, I knew to swerve,
and yet continued riding on, unfazed —
and once it overturned, I just observed:
both th' bridge and cart burn'd up in fiery blaze.
The sight of flames did fill me up with mirth,
like stars within the heavens my soul shares;
yet thou dost try to throw me back to earth
like I've toss'd thy belongings down the stairs.
　　— Indifferent to the rules I've disobeyed,
　　　　I revel in the chaos I have made.

Icona Pop, featuring Charli XCX, "I Love It"

O loyal friend, thou see'est I have dropp'd!
  Thy heart is pure, but do not fear my pain —
for though I may be fell'd, I'll ne'er be stopp'd;
anon I'll rise upon my feet again.
I'll start with whiskey, barman! Then, pray bring
me drams of cider and thy strongest ale!
And whilst I quaff, I'll lift my voice and sing
the whole of Danny Boy's distressing tale!
Although the tune is sad, it doth recall
more pleasant times in days that long since pass'd;
and when the next song echoes through the hall,
it shall our minds to days still better cast.
  — Alas! I find I have been freshly down'd —
    but Life shall never keep me on the ground.

Chumbawumba, "Tubthumping"

The legendary bird of Grecian lore
   shies not away from burning tongues of fire;
it knows beginnings are from endings born
and thus descends onto the fun'ral pyre.
No life or object known upon the Earth
to any other natural law adheres;
the close of day becomes the evening's birth,
when skies reveal the music of the spheres.
To these celestial bodies, raise a toast
for they've maintained a wondrous constancy,
just like we've drifted on Life's trying coasts
too long to any diff'rent sailors be.
  — While ladies dance the night away for sport,
      so we shall, too, their favor sweet to court.

Daft Punk, featuring Pharrell Williams, "Get Lucky"

S ome suitors do believe an earnest kiss
  or soft embrace will let them win my heart;
but if they'll not remit, they are remiss,
for riches are the way to love impart.
Still others try with words to fast endear,
remaining yet too blind to ever see
that my bridegroom shall be my financier;
he'll neither borrower nor lender be.
If costly habit as one's purse can buy,
then each should save their farthings all his life
for purses pursed shall only make me sigh —
a purse dispersed will make a happy wife.
    — If wealthily, then happily when wed,
        I am a girl by want of items led.

Madonna, "Material Girl"

The morning I was born, the midwives smil'd,
rejoicing o'er the cherub they help'd birth.
The eldest cast a sharpen'd eye; the child
she knew delinquent was, not cause for mirth.
'Tis true: a thousand damsels I've distress'd
by granting not the love they did desire;
and still I'll rend true hearts within the breast
of thousands more, ere I this world expire.
My reputation's such that royals cow'r
before me, and good women sinful be;
yet what I want is not within my pow'r:
my loving soul should e'er belong to thee.
— But 'til thy love's declared, it should be known
that I'm a brute, and bad through ev'ry bone.

George Thorogood and the Destroyers,
"Bad to the Bone"

I am a bard; 'tis evening when I rise,
with hopes my soul has woken most inspired —
yet, by the morning when I close my eyes,
I've writ no words; I merely have been tired.
My disenchantment grows with ev'ry move;
this endless sloth does nothing but persist.
I beg thee for the simple chance to prove
that I might stave it off if thou'dst assist.
The flames of inspiration do not burn
from long-dead embers; they must first be stoked.
I have the kindling, but my heart doth yearn
to see thy spark's a raging blaze provok'd.
   — For thee, I would on any quest embark;
      pray, let us dance together in the dark.

Bruce Springsteen, "Dancing in the Dark"

A t break of day, I to my home return'd
to be admonish'd for my entrance late.
O Mother dear, though we're by fortune spurn'd,
its lack will not my want of cheer abate!
When callers to my home at midnight come,
my father asks if I've some long-term plan;
I reassure him he hath not become
the second fiddle to some other man.
Yet that shall not affect the things I do;
my course of life's not plott'd 'round some boy.
When at long last, the day of work is through,
I'll always aim to find my share of joy.
— I'll walk within the sun's enliv'ning rays
for girls just want some fun within their days.

Cyndi Lauper, "Girls Just Want to Have Fun"

My trade is in th' prognosticating arts —
of shifts of wind and climes of farmers' fields;
and I predict — O ladies, steel thy hearts! —
this rising storm shall diff'rent rainfall yield.
It may prepost'rous seem, but I've reread
the evidence and verily assure
the message it originally said:
at ten o'clock, pray get thee out of doors!
Tonight, it shall rain men from ev'ry cloud,
for Mother Nature is a woman, too:
she hath for ev'ry lass a match endow'd,
so find thy handsome fellow to pursue!
   — And when thou'st won thy suitor debonair,
      look up to Heav'n and say a thankful pray'r!

The Weather Girls, "It's Raining Men"

The music I create is quite sublime;
    it makes me thank our Lord in rev'rent pray'r
for blessing me with gifts of wit and rhyme,
as well as shuffling skill beyond compare.
These talents I'll combine to make thee dance;
my rhythms shall persuade thee t'ward the floor
and there, perhaps, thou'lt spark a new romance.
And if my songs should leave thee wanting more,
then ring the school-house bells to class convene
then stop! for now 'tis Hammer's time to teach.
The strains that I have wrought have prov'd obscene
the thought thou couldst my lofty levels reach.
    — Though I have of my craft imparted much,
        my artistry's beyond what thou canst touch.

MC Hammer, "U Can't Touch This"

O sweet and noble lad, be not aggrieved!
  Pray lift thyself from off the cursèd ground!
Thy travels long have left thee most deceived,
for there's a sanctuary to be found.
They've pleasant lodgings for thee at a cost
amenable to one of little wealth,
and pastimes there — too many to exhaust —
to cleanse thy soul and fortify thy health.
Let not thy pride dissuade thee from their aid,
or think I speak of what I do not know;
for in my troubled youth, 'twas there I stay'd
to lift myself from poverty and woe.
  — We've cause to thank them over and again,
    this brotherhood for good young Christian men!

The Village People, "YMCA"

C ome join the sprightly dancing if thou wilt;
  let not the whims of others steer thy course!
Thy friends may be abandon'd without guilt
if they'll not yield to dance's joyous force.
O we can seek some distant foreign shore
where others cannot judge our whimsied ways;
the distance shall permit them to ignore
our wild cavorting, alien and craz'd.
We can in splendid finery be dress'd;
we are allow'd to act the motley fool.
Our merriment hath been with freedom bless'd,
and is unfetter'd by convention's rule.
— Against conformity we will not chafe,
    for here thy chosen dance shall e'er be safe.

Men Without Hats, "The Safety Dance"

The bells toll seven times and I arise;
  my fast is broken with a bowl of gruel.
I freshen up, wash sleep out of my eyes,
and start my daily journey t'ward the school.
My friends approach within a carriage small
and bid I make their trav'ling group complete;
I nod assent, but first must briefly stall
whilst I decide wherein to take my seat.
O Friday, weekend's herald! Happy date,
thy blessèd presence merriment portends!
O harbinger of Sabbath, come elate
our hearts with revelry and time with friends!
  — Thy life began with Thursday's late demise;
    and when thou go'st, sweet Saturday shall rise.

Rebecca Black, "Friday"

I stepp'd from off the ship onto the docks
with naught but fragile hopes and flimsy coat.
I heeded those in rich and frilly frocks
and wanted for their confidences' vote.
My lack of courtly grace brought pangs of fear —
this youthful soul fill'd up with doubt and pain —
'til Night brought blissful music to my ear
and I was calm'd by my most-lov'd refrain.
I lifted up my hands to Heaven's berth
and felt my cower'd courage swiftly steel'd;
my head and heart and hips all moved with mirth —
a fit of gaiety that would not yield.
   — With my resolve renew'd, I now declare
      a celebration in this country fair!

Miley Cyrus, "Party in the USA"

I came to call, late on a Friday eve,
upon my mistress, that she might be woo'd.
I wore a musky fragrance to achieve
a sensuous and amatory mood.
With romance high, we fell in fervid swoons;
we lustily embraced and fondly kiss'd.
Ere long, I found myself sans pantaloons —
and sans regard for our impassion'd tryst.
The lady left, frustrated and annoy'd,
lamenting my misspent attention span.
I've since discover'd people will avoid
a negligent buffoon, more boy than man.
— To act my age I oft have been beseech'd,
    but I cannot recall the age I've reached.

Blink-182, "What's My Age Again?"

'Tis clear I'm not diminutive in size,
　　but I do not lament my shapely curves;
the face of ev'ry gentleman belies
the thrill he feels when he my form observes.
My mother told me I must worry not
about my figure, for each strapping squire
shall grow beneath his collar rather hot —
physiques like mine are what each man desires.
Yet I've seen illustrations drawn in books
by those who would remake my flawless frame.
O, fie on them! I know my girlish looks
exquisite are; their standards are for shame!
　　— To those who would my comeliness embrace,
　　　　thou knowest I am all about that bass.

Meghan Trainor, "All About That Bass"

I spied a boorish rogue across the hall
     whose eyes met mine again in fleeting winks.
Just yesternight, he sought a social call —
he aims to excite jealousy, methinks!
He sits and courts another maiden there
whose vestments are unfashion'ble and coarse.
O, thinkèst thou he finds her visage fair?
Wouldst thou the beauty of her face endorse?
The minstrel's lyrics fill the hall with song:
a story of a love in summer lost.
I find his judgment lacks — the time is wrong,
for summer's heat is still belied by frost.
    — I wish to have a pipe; but first, I'm sure
        I should engage in swift self-portraiture.

The Chainsmokers, "#SELFIE"

From joyous fetes, I'd kept myself aloof
'til one night, struck by music in the air,
I sought its source and found it 'pon a roof:
a spirited soirée beyond compare!
The drums, they rous'd up dancing heaven-sent;
their throbbing tones inspired us to move!
Now was the winter of our disco tent
made glorious summer by this sonic groove.
But as each dancer movèd with the beat,
the rooftop's warmth unbearable became;
we swelter'd in the e'er-increasing heat
and felt we might combust in sudden flame.
— Yet, through the music, I could still discern
a merrymaker speak: "Burn, baby, burn!"

The Trammps, "Disco Inferno"

N ow cease thy talking; prithee, hear my words!
This newly written sonnet I'll recite.
The Muse hath gripp'd my mortal soul and spurr'd
it swiftly forth, just like a spear in flight.
O, will its inspirations ever quit?
I do not know; yet if thou shouldst turn out
the lights herein, I shall a glow emit
and, like a candle, wax a common lout.
It is a crime to not perform thy best,
but greatness is well worth its heavy price.
Pray tell thy mother "word" at my behest —
a missive from the bard Vanilla Ice.
    — If thou hast problems, I'll them all allay;
        now mark the melodies my minstrels play.

Vanilla Ice, "Ice Ice Baby"

By heaven, this was not a plan of mine —
it was no plot or predetermined act.
With courage steel'd by an excess of wine,
I did away with my accustomed tact.
Unbridled curiosity prevail'd;
it bade I peer into a world I'd miss'd.
Of this auspicious moment I avail'd
myself, and I another woman kiss'd.
And such a kiss! The taste of cherry balm
upon her lips was one I'll ne'er forget.
A whirlwind of emotion: craz'd, yet calm —
and hoping my admirer's not upset.
    — But, O! the wond'rous truth I'll not avoid:
        her kiss was one I truly well enjoy'd.

Katy Perry, "I Kissed a Girl"

When thou a week's frustrations must expel,
    thou wishest for a dance hall to unwind;
with plans to seek a suitor there as well,
thy merriment's not all thou hop'st to find.
How music stirs up souls with rhythmic joy!
O, anyone could be thy paramour;
but 'til the right one's found, thou need'st no boy
to frolic free and let thy spirit soar.
Thy sweet exuberance betrays thy youth
for thou art merely seventeen in age;
and yet thy artful movements bare the truth:
thou art a master true upon the stage.
    — All eyes are fix'd upon thee, most entranc'd —
        thy coronation as the Queen of Dance!

ABBA, "Dancing Queen"

PART V

Ballads of
HEROES

Rentus sub alis meis

From western Philadelphia I hail,
    where in my youth I'd play upon the green
'til — rue the day! — I found myself assail'd
by ruffians contemptible and mean.
Although the spat was trivial and brief,
it wounded my dear mother deep within;
and so, to give her conscience sweet relief,
she sent me forth to live amongst her kin.
When to my port of call I'd been convey'd,
I came upon a coachman most unique;
and yet I simply took the trip and paid,
despite his cab's decor and fresh mystique.
    — I survey all the land with princely mien
        in fair Bel-Air, where I do lay my scene.

Will Smith, "The Fresh Prince of Bel-Air"

Long after sunset, patrons shuffle in
to drink away the weary week that's pass'd.
I look about the pub whilst I begin
a ballad sweet, and mark the motley cast.
A wizened man, he asks me for a song
forgotten, though well-lov'd in younger age.
The barkeep swears he doth not here belong,
but dreams instead of glory 'pon the stage.
The sailor and the merchant, they converse —
the wenches flirt — the merchants, they get sous'd.
The tavern-keeper smiles about the purse
he's earnèd from the crowd I've here arous'd.
    — The people cry, "Another tune, anon!
      If music be thy trade, good sir, play on!"

Billy Joel, "Piano Man"

The creak of carriage wheels I long have heard
    but I may never watch their weary turn,
for I'm within this dungeon e'er interr'd
to wait until my soul in Hell shall burn.
My mother taught me morals clear and plain:
the principles to which I should aspire;
yet I've another person coldly slain
in Blackpool, just to watch his life expire.
But I was caught; I must my sentence serve —
and how those axle squeaks fill me with dread:
that I shall nevermore those mares observe
or find a simple pleasure 'til I'm dead!
   — O, if I were from this confinement freed,
      I'd far from prison ride upon that steed.

Johnny Cash, "Folsom Prison Blues"

O stroll about until thou art at rest;
 we wish to bring thy conscience some relief.
To aid our giving calm and comfort best,
pray speak about thy character in brief.
Thy secrets shall into the cupboard go,
beside the pastries and confections sweet.
They're just for elder ministers to know;
we shall around the children be discreet.
Thy soul is precious for its reverent air
as we stand without heroes brave and strong.
Yea, Heaven waits for those who kneel in pray'r,
though pinstrip'd knight hath left and mov'd along.
 — Belovèd by the Lord and Holy Ghost:
  to thee, good Lady Robinson, a toast!

Simon and Garfunkel, "Mrs. Robinson"

My dearest wife, she hath my bags prepared
in readiness, for soon I shall embark
upon a quest to where few men have dared:
I'll venture skyward, high into the dark.
While these crusades must surely rousing seem,
I'll be alone on Icarus's wings —
and while I soar, I've naught to do but dream
about my darling bride and worldly things.
My trek among the stars shall not be brief —
'twill be some time ere o'er the earth I roam;
and when I do, I'll match not thy belief,
for I'm no gallant hero here at home.
   — Such odysseys are how I ply my trade;
      among the spheres, my livelihood is made.

Elton John, "Rocket Man"

One dreary darken'd night upon a ship,
I met a sickly gambl'r clutching dice.
He smok'd my pipe and did my whiskey sip
ere softly smiling, proffering advice.
He said, "I made my way with ev'ry glance,
attending the expressions others wore —
for life is just a larger game of chance,
and reading others helps thee mark the score.
Learn well the time to stay the course thou'st laid,
but know with certitude when thou should'st flee.
Count not thy farthings whilst the game is play'd,
for there'll be time for them to tallied be."
   — With those wise words expir'd the gambling knave;
     though he still lives in th' adages he gave.

Kenny Rogers, "The Gambler"

A way within the southern wooded lands,
there lives a boy of prominent repute;
and though he is unschool'd, he's bless'd with hands
unparalleled in skill for playing lute.
He'd sit along the road, beneath the trees,
to play against the rhythm of the hooves
of passing horses, matching them with ease
as others marvell'd at his joyous grooves.
His mother told him that his talents rare
would bring to him a life of wealth and fame;
'twould let him lead a band of skill'd trouvères
to play beneath marquees that bear his name.
— The criers o'er the land shall thus recite:
"Come hear the songs of John B. Goode tonight!"

Chuck Berry, "Johnny B. Goode"

A dorned in saffron, Lola would enchant
the patrons with her graceful Spanish dance.
Her suitor Tony would their drinks decant
and poured his heart into their sweet romance.
One sordid eve, a wealthy patron came,
accosting Lola in a fashion cruel.
Her stalwart Tony leapt over the bar
to gallantly defend her in a duel.
The vicious battle left the lounge destroy'd,
and sadder still, the brute hath Tony slain.
The bar's now of its storied past devoid —
but Lola and her memories remain.
   — Within its walls, her love was won and lost,
      but learn'd too late the Copa's stars were cross'd.

Barry Manilow, "Copacabana"

One cold November day, we had a feast
made by a kindly friend who owns an inn.
To give my thanks in turn, I thought the least
that I could do was purge her rubbish bins.
I haul'd the refuse, toss'd it from the bluffs
and listened for its landing 'pon the rocks;
'twas then I fell accosted by a gruff
old constable who threw me in the stocks.
Some two years hence, I heard my name be called
from the conscription rolls to serve my Queen;
my crim'nal hist'ry left the sergeants galled,
dismissing me for littering obscene.
　　— So if it's peace thy noble heart should want,
　　　pray, sing of Alice and her restaurant!

Arlo Guthrie, "Alice's Restaurant"

F or thee, they've caravans to sell or lend,
    as well as chambers small where thou canst sleep.
For lodgings, I've no money I can spend;
to earn my stay, I shall the floorboards sweep.
O'er all the land I've roam'd and made my way;
I've vacancies in each vocation fill'd
and kept each precious farthing of my pay,
for ne'er have I subscrib'd to any guild.
I've rarely work'd beyond what's just enough:
my meals are meager, clothes are bare of thread.
Though it may seem my chosen course is rough,
I've revel'd in the life that I have led.
    — I have forgone a permanent abode
        to rule as regent of the open road!

Roger Miller, "King of the Road"

The sun has set — the light of day hath ceased;
the hour of night doth total darkness bring.
Within its shroud, there lies a fearsome beast:
the lion, proud and strong, the jungle's king.
Now that the gates of evening have been broach'd,
there settles o'er the wood a quiet pall —
a sign the fearsome feline hath approach'd
the outskirts of our peaceful village small.
But hush, my sweet! There is no cause for fear;
pray, dry thy eyes! There is no need to weep,
for though the mighty animal is near,
the creature doth already lie in sleep.
　　— Yea, thou art safe; the night is calm and mild —
　　　　so dream away, O dream away, my child!

The Tokens, "The Lion Sleeps Tonight"

There is a southern brothel people call
    the Rising Sun, a place of foul acclaim.
A sordid fate its customers befall;
I know, for mine's among its victims' names.
Although my mother was a seamstress fair —
she sew'd for me these linen pantaloons —
I've follow'd Father's footsteps southward there
to drink down ale and gamble for doubloons.
Yea, men of wayward ilk are ne'er content
unless their throats feel liquor's pleasant burn.
Its haunting beck and call will not relent;
thus to the Rising Sun I'll now return.
    — Pray teach thy children to avert their gaze
        so they may ne'er reprise my sinful ways.

The Animals, "House of the Rising Sun"

Hath this metallic man been render'd mad?
Do his eyes see, or hath his vision laps'd?
Is he adept at walking iron-clad,
or if he moves, will he be found collaps'd?
We know not if he lives, or what's his mind;
his stoic nature lets us him neglect.
Despite his valiant quest to save our kind,
the mission only earn'd him disrespect.
And so he's stood and survey'd all the land;
he lay in wait to loose his brutal force.
By most mechanical and dirty hand,
he rouses up revenge without remorse.
　　— Now those he'd saved retreat in fear and pain;
　　　the vengeful Iron Man doth live again!

Black Sabbath, "Iron Man"

A terror strikes thee at the witching hour
when moonlight's glow reveals some horrid shape.
Such dread doth strike with petrifying pow'r:
thy screams are mute, thy mouth's been left agape.
The only door slams shut — the monster's near —
thine eyes find no escape to thy dismay —
and so they close in agony and fear
as th' awful creature closes on its prey.
There is no recourse from thy star-writ fate;
no hero shall this villain fierce assail —
when suddenly, the onslaught doth abate,
for thou art rous'd from this fantastic tale.
  — I'll thee protect from any storied ghosts,
    for I'm the one who'll thrill thy soul the most.

Michael Jackson, "Thriller"

I drove my carriage o'er the darken'd road
when faintly I observ'd a distant inn.
When I arriv'd, their greeting swift forebode
the vile debauchery I found within.
The cov'tous hostess did for excess pine;
she'd several suitors at her beck and call.
When I appeal'd the captain for my wine,
he said 'twas years since casks were had at all.
He brought me to the mirror'd master room
where all had gather'd to the feast partake.
I ran to leave, but found I'd been entomb'd;
I could not leave, nor e'er my hunger slake.
   — Each night, I hear the concierge repeat
      his welcome as he doth new patrons greet.

The Eagles, "Hotel California"

Is this the waking world, or do I sleep?
I find I can't be rous'd, to my dismay;
but you should not for this delinquent weep
for I'm a brute whose soul's been toss'd away.
O Mother sweet, I bring thee news of dread —
my life's at end, for I've another slain.
I press'd my crossbow up against his head
and loosed its bolt away into his brain.
— but hark! I see a dark and ghostly form
amidst the lightning launch'd by Jove on high!
The cries for mercy, silenced by the storm,
are futile; I'll not be released, but die.
    — My fate now seal'd, 'tis plain for all to see:
        the wind's direction matters not to me.

Queen, "Bohemian Rhapsody"

My stagecoach staidly rumbled 'til I heard
a constable demanding that I halt.
I reined my steeds to heed the watchman's word
when he approach'd and ask'd, "Know'st thou thy fault?"
I question'd, "Is it that I am a Moor?
I am no prophet, sir — pray, state my wrong."
With narrow'd eyes, he spake: "I stopp'd thee for
thy speed excessive whilst thou rode along.
Now from thy cab! I shall thy coach inspect."
"Thou need'st a warrant to my goods besiege."
"A barrister! Still, what might we detect
if we let slip the dogs of law, my liege?"
    — Four score and nineteen problems I possess;
        his bitch, however, brings me no distress.

Jay-Z, "99 Problems"

The curtain falls; my time draws near its end,
  though I shan't fear the bitter wrath of age.
I'll say it clear: I have observ'd, sweet friend,
within my life that all the world's a stage —
and if the men and women players be,
I've played my part with skill, none more the lead.
I've made the most of each soliloquy,
and crafted ev'ry scene to mine own need.
'Tis true, I hold regrets about my past,
but hist'ry stands; I'd never strike it through.
I plott'd out my course, held to it fast,
and as I liked it, spoke my feelings true.
  — And thus, the rest is silence, save to say
    that such a life was mine, lived all my way.

Frank Sinatra, "My Way"

INDEX OF FIRST LINES.

And now, kind readers, here's a thankful word
for Jason, Tom, and Scott's discerning looks:
for both my tireless agents, Sam and Byrd,
and Jonny, who inspired this whole book.
Good Tim and Martin made this tome look great;
Nicole, Suzanne did champion its cause.
I thank the folks at Quirk and th' 4th Estate,
and Julie Stoner's fixing grammar flaws.
Miranda Dubner's edits were divine
and Adam Lurie's brainstorms help'd me write.
The love of friends and fam'ly let me shine
on Tumblr, where these verses first saw light.
  — And last (but not the least) of thanks to say —
    to Becca Bainbridge, th' light in all my days.

Erik Didriksen, "Acknowledgments"

This book was typeset in
IM Fell DW Pica, designed by
Dutch typefounder Peter De Walpergen
under the direction of John Fell (1625-1686),
curator of the Oxford University Press
and Bishop of Oxford. The Fell
typefaces were digitized
by Igino Marini
in 2000.